The Birth Revolution
Poems about birth and parenthood

First Edition: The Birth Revolution - Poems about birth and parenthood

First published in Great Britain in 2022 by
Rose Garden Press.

Simon Jackson has asserted his right under the Copyright, Designs and Patents Act 1988 to be identified as the author of this work.

Simon Jackson © 2022

ISBN: 9798359361552

Designed and typeset in Palatino Linotype by Rose Garden Press.

Cover design © Simon Jackson & Ali Hayes 2022

Rose Garden
Press 2022

Simon Jackson was the director of Living Arts Space Theatre Company for several years. He then became an itinerant musician, journalist and teacher in East Europe, North Africa, South America, Scotland and South East Asia.

He writes poetry, plays, short stories and music, all of which have won awards. His short films have been screened by the BBC and internationally. None of this has ever come close to making him a living but goes a long way to alleviating boredom.

Born in Manchester, Simon now lives in Shanghai with his wife, daughter and son, teaching Film and Art in an International School and leading his jazz-punk band, Hogchoker, who were invited to play Glastonbury in 2019.

https://www.hogchoker.net

But that's another story.

Photo Philippe Roy Kore Studios

Praise for *The Birth Revolution*

"An impressive and beautiful sequence of finely-wrought poetry charting the wonder, pain, anxiety, humour and utter joy of the early journey of fathering."
Berlie Doherty, twice winner of the Carnegie Medal, and the Writers Guild of Great Britain Award

"In these direct, skilful and moving poems, Simon Jackson does the near impossible, conjuring up the trinity of love, despair and exhaustion that is parenting. At the centre of the story he puts the mother's visceral experience, as any sane father does. Recommended for old parents who want to recall their experiences, and new parents who want to feel less lonely, and soon-to-be parents who need to prepare for what is about to hit them."
Mike Stocks, winner of the Goss First Novel Award

"Before cards, toys, babygrows, nappy cream, prams or blankets, you should buy this tender, thought-provoking collection for anyone who is expecting, has children or was ever a child. Humane, life-affirming and full of joy and wonder, this is a collection the world needs right now."
Tom Brodie, The British Council

Praise for Jackson's previous collection, *Fragile Cargo*

"These poems offer… a casual musicality, tenderly-scrutinizing love poems, the inevitability of loss and the possibility of recovery. I particularly like their unapologetic vulnerability, unprotected by smartness or irony; they don't give themselves airs – they just deliver."
Andrew Greig, poet, playwright, novelist and mountaineer, winner of the Eric Gregory Award and Saltire Scottish Book of the Year

"Jackson is a brave poet. There's an underlying tenderness to Fragile Cargo, but the poems are all written with such energy and bite that the reader is never allowed to feel comfortable. They're funny too. More please."
Mark Wallington, author, TV and film writer

"From the incisively observational to the profoundly moving and all shades in-between; a collection of gems."
Caroline Dunford, author and playwright, including the Euphemia Martins detective series

"Having read my first Simon Jackson poem I wanted to read the next… well crafted, thought provoking and, above all, enjoyable and will leave you wanting more."
Tony Gutteridge, Grace Dieu Writers' Awards

"Whether dealing with work, family, desire or the nature of belief, these poems focus, in vivid detail, on the point of contact between the known and unknowable, the wished-for and the feared."
Dilys Rose, winner of two Scottish Arts Council Book Awards and the Canongate Prize

The Birth Revolution
Poems about birth and parenthood

by
Simon Jackson

Acknowledgments

My grateful thanks to the editors and sponsors of the following
publications, anthologies and awards where these poems have
appeared: *Agenda, ASP Zine* (China), *The Brown Review* (India), *The
Dawntreader, Feile-Festa* (US), *HQ Poetry, The Journal, Kith Review,
Poetry Plus, Obsessed by Pipework, The Reading Hour* (India) and the
anthology *New Beginnings* (Reynard Press).

Cosmonaut was awarded 2nd place in the Onward Poetry
Competition, *Sleep Training* won 1st place in The Poetry Hut Poetry
Contest and *Building a Box* was awarded 1st place in the Grace Dieu
Poetry Awards.

Many thanks to my bandmates and collaborators,
to Berlie Doherty, Mike Stocks and Mark Wallington for
encouragement, advice and edits,
and to my Mum, Caroline, my editor, proofreader
and accomplice.

*Dedicated to everyone bold enough to embark upon that
wonderful, terrifying adventure called parenthood*

*and to the loves of my life,
my beautiful children, Bella and Max,
and their mother, Jana.*

CONTENTS
Part I - The Birth Revolution

Part II - Birth and Revolution

Part III – poems from *Fragile Cargo*

Part I

The Birth Revolution
Poems of birth and parenthood

A Charm Against Drowning

Trees carry the pulse of running water
in their leaves, a memory
of their birth and nourishment
just as the dark of womb and drum
of mothers' heartbeat rush in our ears
when we close our eyes at night

Tadpoles

Again, I've been scooping up the stuff of life.
A jam-jar rubs against my groin,
filled, hopefully, with swarming tadpoles
too tiny for the eye to see,
keeping the sample body temp
as I cycle to the clinic.

Awaiting is not a bowl in my window
but petri-dish and pipette.

Across the years my eight-year old self
cycles excitedly beside me,
impatient for his jar of slippery spawn
to mutate into writhing life.

Unborn

I am secret
I am your secret
hidden even to you

a twinkle inside
planted roughly in your galaxy
a star's reflection in warm salt sea

this clumsy grapple
this tangle of limbs
this fumble of falling clothing

this hungry suckling
these greedy mouths joining
this hot panting

moaning like wounded animals
this seed of new beginning
is this love?

I am unexpected
still unknown
something shocking

you will know me first
as a sickness then a hunger
and a slow swelling

all I know is this warm sea
this lifeline anchoring me
to your heartbeat

I am adrift in a capsule
round as the moon
pulling the tides behind me

I travel hopefully trusting my line
will hold firm until arrival
one cord stretching to the curved sail

a billowing spinnaker before me
a gentle thunder pulsing around
like breaking waves, the surge of surf

I am the piece of grit
hoping to become a pearl

Science Fiction

It looks like a sci-fi feature,
a slim spacecraft approaching,
now piercing, the atmosphere
of a bulging planet's sphere.

This room could be a rocket's cockpit,
the gleaming dials and gauges,
the screens, the shining chrome.
The instruments are sharp and strange
as alien weaponry.

Our pilot guides a needle-sharp craft
between your parted legs.
We watch the progress on the screen
awaiting signs of touchdown,
all eagerly hoping he'll return
with tidings of newly discovered life.

Screen Test

A whir of electronics
and your face lights up the silver screen,
each shining, grainy particle
a magnet, drawing us in.

We are transfixed. You have star quality.

We crane forward
to catch your tiniest motion,
are filled with joy at the hint of a smile.
I can see right into your heart,
and mine leaps, speeds up
to almost match your own.

You exist in a different world to us.
No worries of paying a monthly mortgage,
fed and watered, chauffeur driven,
floating in your private galaxy.

The screening ends.
As the lights rise and the screen goes blank
I note with surprise that my eyes are damp.
I help my wife off the hospital bed.
We leave the ward clutching a print out
of your image and plan a reception
worthy of Oscar night
to celebrate your advent.

Still Picture

In the glow of the moving, sepia scan
you smiled at me and in your face
I saw the features of you, my child,
I saw my son to be; could read
the twitching visage, comprehend
clear expressions, see the character
of a person I soon would know.

Now, staring at the monochrome
print I feel I have lost you, son,
I cannot find you in the black-grey smudge
that was your face; instead I see
a shadowed death mask filmed
within the coffin's shade;
I see my dad's decaying corpse,
smudged and indistinct and fading.

This frozen image holds nothing
of you, or the future you,
or future generations.
It is a smeary salt print
of my rotting ancestry
and of my own approaching destiny.

You care not for photographs.
You kick, vital, pulsing, living,
in technicolour motion
in the globe of my wife's belly.

Cosmonaut

Tiny cosmonaut, you travel
uncharted voyages in your mother ship,
attached by a skyblue lifeline
you chart the light of passing stars.

Each encounter a fleeting enigma
as you map the dark galaxies
by sound filtered through
the pulsing spaceship's hull.

You float in suspended animation,
slowly rotating as the months count down,
your capsule bulging out of shape.
You expand with your universe

as you grow ever nearer your destination,
unaware of the life-changing impact
your landing will have on the starry-eyed inhabitants
of the world where you touch down.

Moon

I am the waxing moon.
Expressionless. Holder of secrets.
Each day a little fatter, rounder,
swollen with my keepsake.
Someone soon must squint and stare
and spot with shock the transformation.
I stroke my ballooning white flesh,
extending to fill my whole horizon.
Many moons will pass
before I wane to a pale, slim crescent.

On the Verge

Your body is caterpillar fat.
Liquid layers cocoon the baby within.
You are a chrysalis, wrapped from the inside.
Expectant yet fearful
as to what you will become.
How you will be changed.
Your round body rocking,
Teetering on the edge,
Your pendulous walk ticking off the days
And drawing stares and smiles that tell
You can no longer pass as one of the girls;
Not yet a mother.

Geography

Seismic forces have upturned the topography
of your body and I'm left without the tools
or means to map or measure them.
The undulating desert sands of stomach,
the gentle dunes of breasts are unrecognizable.

No storm has thrown these new contours,
no ice-age calving fresh arêtes,
peaks and troughs, alluvial ridges,
nor ocean waves sculpting vast cliffs.

Your new form is perfect, not forced by fault-lines'
friction, the heat of new life bubbling
is the furnace that forges this mountain,
smooth and warm as fresh-blown glass,
miraculous as a new-formed star.

Earth Magic

Ancient signs foretell the blood will cease its flow, stagnate
and when again it comes a gory lake will fill, then flood, then
gush;
the flat earth shudders, starts to swell, fresh tumuli rise, the bones
beneath
come together, leeched from clay, subterranean caverns hiss
new conduits open, waters trill, prehistoric magic flows,
salts and mineral coalesce, form twitching muscle from the loam
the coffin walls sigh and flex, beneath the earth the buried groan.

The moon which melted to a blade of grass now ripens, melon fat,
now sickens, wastes until pip thin, repeats four times, then four
again.
Ancient rites prepare the ground for earthquake, lava, this fresh
miracle
but no liturgy can tell the wonder when the ground will break,
the stone will crack and roll away, a flood, renaissance, Genesis,
new life tastes the stale, grey air, takes breath in unique inspiration
mightier than any god or magic thrills this pulse of new creation.

Portophobia

They'd call me phobic
if they knew my fear of doors.
I refuse. I don't want to come out.

Even if I turn my back it's there.
A swirling vortex, a black hole,
A vacuum, a drain, a plug hole
About to suck me down,
A gaping maw waiting to devour.

It may seem an over reaction.
It's only a gateway, a simple egress,
A portal to another room.

To me it is the unknown.
It is the end of comfort and safety.
The noises from the other side
Are the sounds of torture and terrible creatures.

They plan to drag me out.
Force me with drugs and forceps and gloved hands
To the bright lights, the white coats…

I'll keep clinging to the warm, smooth walls,
To the pulsing beat of my room.

Preparation

Cleaning hands, boiling water,
laying out shining utensils
as if for Sunday dinner.

The guests stand expectantly
around the well baked offering
impatient to be served.

Almost ready;
aprons on, rubber gloves
as if to wash up.

At last. How can the dish
look so undercooked
after so very long in the oven?

Bloody, pale flesh,
creased and folded as if wrapped
too tight, too long in cling film.

We consume him
with our eyes, with our smiles
with our relief and our love.

With our hunger.

Broken Water

Your limbs, fish belly pale
beneath shivering water
eyes wide, black as an orca's fin.
A flush of blood.
Sudden carmine cumulo-nimbus.
Darker matter hangs in clumps
like sodden bread.
Fear circles, flashing a fin.

Your face contorts, twists to scream.
Your body convulses again. Again.
And as the threshing waters' alpine peaks subside
calm hands reach down,
separate one pulsing life into two
and lift our daughter into virgin air.

A Holy Trinity

A flash of blood, primal red in the birthing pool
led to our unplanned arrival in this ward.
The doctors: mechanics, engineers,
talking in cubic centimetres,
poking and prodding, twisting with steel instruments,
following a set of blueprints in lights as bright as an arc welder.

You were an artist.
You stroked my wife's brow, marble white,
as if she were a priceless sculpture,
called for analgesia, painting over the hurt
in wide, wet brush stokes,
leaving only a blurred wash of pain.
You lowered the lights and raised my spirits
and let her rest, the canvas primed.

When you delivered my daughter,
her body blue-white,
for an instant my heart stopped.
You moulded life and colour into her putty limbs,
delivered her into my wife's arms,
a breathing, screaming work of art
and I loved all three of you
far more than anything I've felt for a paternal trinity.

The Light

You are composed of heavenly light and shade,
arms raised like Caravaggio's Saint Paul
in his Conversion on the Road to Damascus.
Your hands reach into the surgeon's light.
I am relegated to the shadows
like Saul's servant, holding the horse's head,
a role of unenlightened comforter,
as you focus, blind to all else,
fingers raised as if blessing,
beckoning the light of our daughter
into this world.

A Grand Entrance

We could not have been more delighted with your debut.
There was not a dry eye in the house.
We are your audience, your critics,
your producers, directors, authors.
Even the stagehand a role to play,
her deft fingers repairing the tear
that gave you an entrance into this world.
Exhausted by your premiere
you recline against your mother's breast,
murmur a monologue of milky burps.

Delivery

The wise men stand up, step back,
present offerings of advice, reassurances
of health, of weight, of length.

Their gift is already with us,
washed, wiped, wrapped
and delivered.

The Munificence of Nature
to an Astonished New Father

Your breasts are magnificent, twin cupolas, domes,
resistant to gravity as hot air balloons,
zeppelins, jelly moulds, jellies, full mixing bowls,
munificent, other-worldly capsules,
unreal as the airbrushed globes in sci-fi,
rock albums, centrefolds, video games,
pumped with silicon, uranium, helium,
and I wonder why we boys, since school,
find so appealing an anatomy
that in nature only ever appears in
a breastfeeding, unimpregnateable lady.
An aspiration to not burrow back in
to the womb, or even to its admission,
but desire to aspire to the situation
of being mothered in perpetuation.

Newborn

Lying tiny in our double bed
between the eyelids of duvet and pillow
you are now the iris that is
the colour in our lives,
the pupil through which we see.

Our vision is transformed
into the shades and shapes you react to.
You reach to the light with a moth's divination
clutching doll like hands as if to grasp it,
turn your head to sounds beyond our intuition.
We struggle to read your body's semaphore and provide
before your entire being wracks into an anguished shriek of need.

Everything we are has been sublimated to our new roles;
worshippers, acolytes, priests, martyrs, sacrifices
to your dogma, inscrutable Buddha,
pure, unsullied by life,
complex beyond our comprehension.
Your body writhes like burning paper.

We strive to decipher the tea leaf patterns you leave,
blessed by their passage through your entrails.
We are soothsayers dedicated to reading the auguries
left in your defecation,
oracles pronouncing your thoughts and feelings
to the tribe of friends and relatives who coo, nod and return
from their pilgrimage satisfied, wiser, to pass on their revelations.

Failed Poem on New Parents' Similes

The hair on my baby's head is as soft as…
My baby's fingers are as intricate as…
My baby is as lovely as…

No, at this moment there is nothing
as soft as the hair on my baby's head,
as intricate, magical, as perfectly formed
as her tiny fingers, nothing,
nothing as lovely.

Dreams of Newness

What do you dream of, little one,
when you lie there, legs kicking as you cycle
through the stratosphere, snuffling like a hog
rooting through drifts of crisp autumn leaves
as you search for truffles on the forest floor,
snorting like a dragon about to expel
a roasting plume of flame,
growling like a lion warning off a young rival
or honking like a flock of geese
chasing the stork that could have delivered you?

Where have you found this menagerie of sound
to add to the bird-like chirrups
and mousey squeaks
and screams that send the seagulls fleeing
in your few days on this planet?

Metamorphosis

When I awoke I found I had become
a worker grub, unable
to lift my body from the ground
foraging to feed the smaller queen
that inches along beside me.
I do not sleep.
I am blind. An insect being of the earth
I see nothing of the world that I used to know.
I am white and soft. I am pulp, mucus.
I follow secretions, a trail of need.
I exist only to bring you nourishment,
responding only to your calls.
Nature has ordained this.
How can I do otherwise?
We are one linked pupa
inside a great, dark cocoon.

But as you start to spread your wings,
emerge from your chrysalis
of nappies and swaddling
so I too feel a delicate flutter
flexing beneath my stained shirt
and I flit with you from flower to flower
that I hadn't even noticed were growing
around our bedroom, seeing the world
with fresh eyes, with antennae
that have sprouted fresh beneath my muffled form.

Sleep Training

You lie so at ease in my arms,
a dead weight, a lamb's pelt, a whole sirloin,
and yet as I lower you into your cot
your body stiffens, your breathing stutters,
shunts from smooth curve of hill and dale
to jagged peaks and sudden drops
of Cairngorm summits, Grampian pinnacles.

Every time I leave, her peaceful form rises,
grasps the prison bars of her cot
and screams her tiny lungs out.
She is Captain Ahab on the prow,
calling to his great adversary from across the globe's oceans,
Prometheus chained, regretting fiercely the gift he gave
as the eagle tears his entrails loose.

Your mother weeps in our bed
as the clarion call summons me back
to sit for hours by your side,
powerless to sleep, afraid to leave,
that you will feel the lack of me.

I stroke your beautiful head,
the wisps of hair lain on your neck,
are soft and warm and delicate as woodsmoke.

You seem so at peace.
Only your breath gives you away.
A pause before each exhalation
as if stopping to listen for prowling wolves,
as if on the point of a cry of panic.

You sense the second I rise to my feet
but will sleep at peace, almost at peace,
for hour after hour as I scribble verse

46

or read my book in the sightless eye
of this bicycle light, a beacon
guiding us through this long night together.

Magician

Magician, no magic wand,
your enchantment a gappy grin
and a wave of a yoghurt coated hand,
and you turn full grown adults
into gurning fools, a monkey band
chimping for your amusement,
mindless flotsam
bobbing on your smile.

A cruel magic it is,
to demean these once-proud creatures,
strip them of dignity
as a jealous God his wandering worshippers,
a vengeful khan his rebellious slaves,
to make them jesters in front of their king,
TV contestants crushed beneath
the weight of the camera lens' gaze.

My Baby the Drunkard

You wobble across the room, giggling,
burst into raucous laughter
with no discernible provocation,
then swing suddenly for my face,
catching me below the eye.
You lose balance and fall.
I notice you've been sick on yourself.
As I wipe you clean you fall asleep,
sprawled across my shoulder.

Three Ages

Lying curled against your mother's belly
you are a fairground mirror's image,
mother to daughter; each one
an undulating sea of smooth curves.

Daughter facing son, face to face,
unaware of the other's existence,
one out, one still within
a before and after shot

or a cut away section
in a medical textbook;
mother and child and child to be
a vision of past, present and future,

Klimpt's *Three Ages* painted in
the afternoon sun's gold,
the window's shadow framing and patterning
what was, is, and what will be

and I am overwhelmed by such love for the three of you,
I am shocked to sudden tears
and leave the room blinking them back
before you get concerned and ask me

what is wrong?
and I'm forced to admit
that for once, there is nothing;
everything is absolutely, perfectly right.

Part II
Birth and Revolution

Poems written during the Arab Spring and the subsequent years of coup, struggle and disappointment

After Bella was born in our one-bedroom apartment in Edinburgh we bought a larger, more expensive flat. When we, unexpectedly, were expecting her brother, Max, we realised we wouldn't be able to pay the mortgage on the new place during maternity leave. My wife, Jana, had interned at the United Nations in Cairo during her MA in Arabic and Spanish and loved the city. I took a job in the British International School of Cairo that included free housing and we rented out our new home without ever living there.

Cairo is where Max was born, in a private clinic overlooking the Nile, and where the following poems were written, caught up in the revolution of child raising and the rebellion of the Arab Spring and its aftermath.

Birth and Revolution

Talk. Years of talk.
Years of talking and planning.
Such dissatisfaction at how we are.

We need change,
We must progress before
everything beautiful in us dies,
move our strictured state forward
to usher in the next stage.

The first attempts are failures,
but we are exhilarated
at trying to shape the future;
we demonstrate daily,
hoping the grappling excitement
of the instant will change our existence.

At last, something is growing.
germinating, a fresh spring
taking root.

Almost a year maturing
and the final, anguished hours are here;
the concentrated push,
the screams, the tearing of flesh,
the tortured face, the blood –
so much more than I expected.

We cling to our prize, born from us,
of our will, our flesh,
a miracle, beyond beauty or price.
Laceratingly tiny and vulnerable;
feeble, almost blind;
mouth gulping unfamiliar air,
hands grasping without strength to hold.

He cannot feed, much less stand, alone.

No-one is prepared for the ceaseless vigilance
we first time parents need
to ensure a newborn keeps drawing breath.

Birth in a Dictatorship - Proposals for an Instillation

A desert dune pyramid.
One green bud
tongues through skin coloured sand.

*

A dark lighthouse crumbling beneath the storm.
In the mountainous, dark waves
a bright red child's toy bobs merrily.

*

A circuit of lights
joined to the power source
by one polished band of copper.

*

A broken fist of coal.
A toe nail of diamond
glints inside.

*

A dry, dead oak, striated and twisted.
In the light seeping through the broken branches
a pale shoot quivering under a light rain.

The first child is a dictatorship

The first child is a dictatorship.
The second is a civil war.

The dictatorship is heralded in
by blood and screaming.
The motherland is wracked by pain,
convulses in her agony
but is reborn, becomes new,
transforms into her unfamiliar role.
At once the dictatorship asserts her position.
Her appetites must be sated.
There can be no discussion.

The next revolution is preceded
by long discussion on how
the new manifestation will be;
consultation on the name,
the roles, the inevitable change
ballooning into our nation.
The birth pains seem more bearable;
this was our choice, and yet
they issue in the civil war.

Birth of Max vs Death of Cleopatra

*For my son, Maksim, born in Cairo, 31.12.12 at the end of the Arab
Spring Rebellions*

She died in August and was taken down the Nile
You were born on New Year's Eve beside the Nile's breaking
waters

A nation stopped and mourned
A nation stopped to celebrate

She took a poisoned asp to her breast
You were taken at once to your mother's breast

She bathed in asses milk
You were bathed then suckled mother's milk

She was loved by Caesar and Mark Anthony
You are deeply loved by your Mother and me

She died and ended the wars of succession
You are born into ongoing revolution

Open Wound

Child,
You are an open wound.
Your screams bring torture,
rape and murder into my bedroom.

Child,
You are an open wound.
The scrape of being leaves nothing as abstract as before or after,
only the shriek of NOW NOW NOW!

Child,
You are an open wound.
The first discomfort and you screech for its cessation.
The first stroke of pleasure and you squeal in delight
at the instant balm.

We swaddle ourselves in bandages
so thick we feel nothing through their dry skin.
We slice ourselves to the bone
on unchecked ambition,
self-castigation,
and unreciprocated love
just to feel anything at all.

Child,
You are an open wound.
We scream together at this world's injustice.

A Curfew of Children

The endless tedium of child rearing,
despite constant crises and emergencies,
is much like life under military rule.

A strict curfew keeps us in at night,
in fact, fear of the consequences involved in leaving
the flat keep us sequestered within all day.

The oppression can feel endless;
our daily activities dictated
by a force outside ourselves.

There is danger. There are tragedies.
Max slipped on the marble floor and bruised his head.
51 protesters were shot dead trying to enter Tahrir Square.

Bella fell off her scooter, racing along the entrance hall.
Our French friend, Eric, was picked up after curfew
and beaten to death in a prison cell.

Each horrifying, external event
shocks briefly but does little to change
the politics of our existence,

unlike the rule of our mini mullahs
who dictate our whole system of belief and being.

Making Love in a Time of War

How can you make love in a time of war?
We no longer even try.
Accepting the wail of incoming mortars
will take out our bed, our nude, writhing bodies,
in one shriek of incessant, anguished need;
that trenches, minefields, barricades
have been already dug, planted, raised
between us; that the screaming maimed
must always be salved before we tend
to ourselves, fix breakages, lick our wounds.

How can you make love in a time of war?
We no longer even try.
But perhaps if we did our forces would pause,
feel this is not a war at all
and wonder why we've been fighting a peace.

Part III

Poems from
Fragile Cargo

My Fever
(for Jana)

Confined to bed, sheets sticking
like shrink wrap to my fevered skin.
The sun seeps in through the curtains like a stain.

The sweet sharpness of peppers, hung in chains outside
to make *ajvar*, or *kiseli paprika*
and keep us the whole winter, fills the room.

Mushrooms are drying on the straw
and my mother's voice rises from the thick walled kitchen
as she stirs the chicken soup to nurse me to health.

I know you're dead. I know this country
doesn't even exist anymore,
yet the smell of fresh linen and *rakija*

rubbed onto my boyish breast
enwraps me more convincingly
than this new land or duvet that weigh upon me now.

Baba putting wet oats in my socks
to take away the fever,
mother scolding her home-spun remedies.

I feel my mother's hand, warm and dry,
passing across my fevered forehead
and know that all will be well.

Sgriob

On days so cold the woolly hanks
of passers breath are left when they have gone,
snagged upon the barbs of frozen air,
and auguries of glazed puddles
lend a window
to the mottled bone and shadow
of an impending underworld,
and ghostly sheep led home for long nights
are lost between the mist of field
and their own breath's fog,
on a day such as this the Gaelic shepherds
coined a word unique to their tongue –
sgriob, a term rich in anticipation
describing the itch on the upper lip
before the inaugural sip of the water of life,
that very first whiskey of the day.

Building a Box

He planes the maple in long smooth sweeps
of his joiner's hands.

Shavings rise like smoke
and tumble in a wave-break
of scattered curls below,
crisp and delicate as shells.

In my hands they are
warring scorpions, drifting leaves,
a cascading avalanche.

I am shooed away with hands
huge as oak trees.

The sky is wooden.
Clouds curl in whorls of grain
around a knot of sun.

He carves hidden joints and panels with
chiselled thumbs,
fingers blunt as hammers.

He pieces together
a box perhaps
a mastless boat. It seems
a simple puzzle for such hours of sweat;
his face is gleaming, head bent.

Slow hands build wood dark with wax,
sail the surface in tiny circles
concealing deeper maps of grain.

He will not come and join me
on the big stone table from where I

set sail to distant lands

or let me ride the tempest
of his hurricane shoulders
about the yard.

I watch. Waiting.

He takes me
shell like
to his warm ship of body
and sorrow breaks
over him like a wave.

It seems a small vessel to hold six
months of baby sister.

Lifejacket

Something untouchable has changed in the darkness of the room,
like the hush of rain edging in or the clock's ticking suddenly
ceasing.

We embrace as if we would meld like putty into one,
closer than we ever were through months pretending this could be
love

held close by the acceptance there is nothing to keep us together
and tomorrow we will drift, alone.

I cling to you as if you are the one imperished lifejacket
on this vast, empty ocean.

Sex Ed

Male and female physiology.
Sexual reproduction in mammals.
Pre-natal development. Child birth.
I circle my hand
and enclose the uneven writing
in a chalk placenta.

"That is the scope of these lessons.
Anything outside this circle
will not be discussed."
And then, trying to hold back
a shiver of nerves:
"Any questions?"

Embarrassed silence, glowing cheeks,
eyes furtively flicking from rubber
to pencil to sharpener and back,
each endowed with symbolic significance.
Then one arm, extending erect:

"Sir, is it true what me sister told me?
She said that when her mate did it..."
and another arm, extending slowly as a snail's antler,
and another, gently waving until
the class is an opened sea anemone.

"I heard if you done it standing up..."
"Sir, why do people do it?"
"Does it go up the same hole a lady pees from?"
"Sir, does it hurt a lot?"

All these nervous, giggling, embarrassed faces,
each shining with eagerness to know
the secret rites of this arcane, adult world.

"Sir, do you and your wife, y'know,
do you and your wife still do it?"

When did our bodies cease to be
a solemn, magical mystery to each other,
become mundane, disorderly and vaguely embarrassing?
Once more I motion to the board.

"These questions are outside the circle."

Rose Garden
Press 2022

Printed in Great Britain
by Amazon

13083714R00047